Meow!

ISBN-13: 978-1-60553-249-3
ISBN-10: 1-60553-249-5

If Kittens Could Talk

Purr and Simple

Written by Dana Bottenfield

new seasons®

Did she just ask me to fetch something?

The audacity...

I have dominated my opposition.

Kitten. Knitten.

If one more person says

"hang in there, baby …"

Yes, this is an
excellent vintage…
room temperature
with a hint of catnip.

What **is** that?

There are no feathers. No bells.

What do you **do** with it?

Yes. I'm pouting.

Curiosity is thought on

its entering edge.

—Charles H. Parkhurst

In hindsight, this wasn't a good idea.

I know the answer!

The puppy did it!

If I could just figure out
how to turn it on,
I could rule the world.

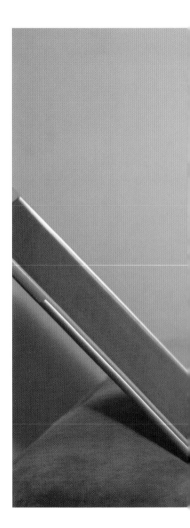

Curiosity did what to the cat?

Now I have you in my clutches!

It has been the providence of
nature to give this creature
nine lives instead of one.

—Pilpay

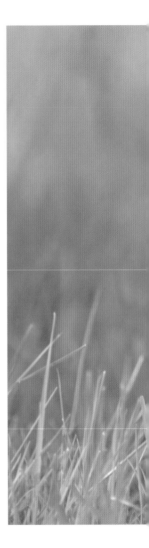

I guess this is what she meant by time out.

I swear the fish was **this** big!

Catnap in my cat hammock.

Kitten attack!

Puss in boot!

A true friend is forever a friend.

—George MacDonald

I'm sorry that I'm cuter than you.

Enjoy the honey-heavy dew of slumber.

—Shakespeare

Hello, lunch.

You missed a spot.

Does this fur make me look fat?

Your feathery antics are no match for my feline prowess!

This stuff comes in a glass?

Intriguing…

Patience is the art of hoping.

—Vauvenargues

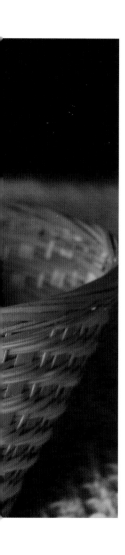

Ok. So I might be a scaredy-cat.

I must show the leafy vine who's boss!

Born to be fuzzy.

My. Toys.

Not. Yours.

To be loved, be loveable.

— Ovid

What is THAT?

So this is what the other side looks like!

Whatcha got there?